Born in 1998

by

Kerry Butters.

Born in 1998

Millennium: 2nd millennium

Centuries: 19th century – **20th century** – 21st century

Decades: 1960s 1970s 1980s – **1990s** – 2000s 2010s 2020s

Years: 1995 1996 1997 – **1998** – 1999 2000 2001

1998 (MCMXCVIII) was a common year starting on Thursday (dominical letter D) of the Gregorian calendar, the 1998th year of the Common Era (CE) and *Anno Domini* (AD) designations, the 998th year of the 2nd millennium, the 98th year of the 20th century, and the 9th year of the 1990s decade.

1998 was designated as:

International Year of the Ocean

Contents

Events

January

- January 2 – Russia begins to circulate new rubles to stem inflation and promote confidence.
- January 4 – Wilaya of Relizane massacres of 4 January 1998 in Algeria: Over 170 are killed in 3 remote villages.
- January 6 – The Lunar Prospector spacecraft is launched into orbit around the Moon, and later finds evidence for frozen water, in soil in permanently shadowed craters near the Moon's poles.
- January 8 – Ramzi Yousef is sentenced to life in prison for planning the first World Trade Center bombing in 1993.
- January 11 – Over 100 people are killed in the Sidi-Hamed massacre in Algeria.
- January 12 – Nineteen European nations agree to forbid human cloning.
- January 14 – Ralph Guarino is arrested for attempting to rob a Bank of America bank in the World Trade Center.

- January 17 – The *Drudge Report* breaks the story about U.S. President Bill Clinton's alleged affair with Monica Lewinsky, which would lead to the House of Representatives' impeachment of him.
- January 20 – Nepalese police intercept a shipment of 272 human skulls in Kathmandu
- January 22 – Suspected "Unabomber" Theodore Kaczynski pleads guilty, and accepts a sentence of life without the possibility of parole.
- January 28 – Gunmen hold at least 400 children and teachers hostage for several hours, at an elementary school in Manila, Philippines.

New rubles

Lunar Prospector

February

- February – The United States Senate passes Resolution 71, urging U.S. President Bill Clinton to "take all necessary and appropriate actions to respond to the threat posed by Iraq's refusal to end its weapons of mass destruction programs".
- February 3 – Cavalese cable car disaster: a United States military pilot causes the deaths of 20 people near Trento, Italy, when his low-flying plane severs the cable of a cable-car.
- February 4 – The 5.9 Mw Afghanistan earthquake shakes the Takhar Province with a maximum Mercalli intensity of VII (*Very strong*). With 2,323 killed, and 818 injured, damage is considered extreme.
- February 7–22 – The 1998 Winter Olympics are held in Nagano, Japan.
- February 16 – China Airlines Flight 676 crashes into a residential area near Chiang Kai-shek International Airport, killing 202 people (all 196 on board and 6 on the ground).
- February 20 – Iraq disarmament crisis: Iraqi President Saddam Hussein negotiates a deal with U.N. Secretary General Kofi Annan, allowing weapons inspectors to return to Baghdad, preventing military action by the United States and Britain.
- February 28 – A massacre in Likoshane, FR Yugoslavia starts the Kosovo War.

March

- March 2
  - Data sent from the Galileo probe indicates that Jupiter's moon Europa has a liquid ocean under a thick crust of ice.
  - In Austria, Natascha Kampusch is abducted by Wolfgang Přiklopil (she will remain in his captivity until August 2006).
- March 5 – NASA announces that the Clementine probe orbiting the Moon has found enough water in polar craters to support a human colony and rocket fueling station.
- March 11 – Danish parliamentary election, 1998: Prime Minister Poul Nyrup Rasmussen is re-elected.
- March 13 – The High-Z Supernova Search Team becomes the first team to publish evidence that the universe is expanding at an accelerating rate.
- March 23 – The 70th Academy Awards ceremony, hosted for the 6th time by Billy Crystal, is held at the Shrine Auditorium in Los Angeles, California. *Titanic* wins 11 Oscars including Best Picture.
- March 24 – First Computer-assisted Bone Segment Navigation, performed at the University of Regensburg, Germany.
- March 26 – Oued Bouaicha massacre in Algeria: 52 people are killed with axes and knives; 32 of the killed are babies under the age of 2.
- March 31 – Netscape released Mozilla source code under an open source license. This is described in The Book of Mozilla, 3:31.

April

Akashi-Kaikyo Bridge

- April 5 – In Japan, the Akashi Kaikyō Bridge linking Shikoku with Honshū and costing about US$3.8 billion, opens to traffic, becoming the largest suspension bridge in the world.
- April 6 – Pakistan tests medium-range missiles capable of hitting India.
- April 10 – Good Friday: 1 hour after the end of the talks deadline, the Belfast Agreement is signed between the Irish and British governments and most Northern Ireland political parties, with the notable exception of the Democratic Unionist Party.
- April 20 – The alleged date the German Red Army Faction (created 1970) is dissolved.
- April 22 - Disney's Animal Kingdom opens at Walt Disney World in Orlando, Florida
- April 23 – The Yugoslav Army ambushes a group of Kosovo Liberation Army fighters attempting to smuggle weapons from Albania into Kosovo, killing 19.

May

- May 8 – CBS telecasts *The Wizard of Oz* for the last time. Beginning in 1999, *The Wizard of Oz* will be shown on cable, and in 2002, 2003, 2004, and 2005 it will be telecast by the WB Television Network in addition to its cable showings.

- May 11
  - India conducts 3 underground nuclear tests in Pokhran, including 1 thermonuclear device.
  - The first euro coins are minted in Pessac, France. Because the final specifications for the coins were not finished in 1998, they will have to be melted and minted again in 1999.
- May 13–14 – Riots directed against Chinese Indonesians break out in Indonesia. Indonesian natives destroy and burn Chinese Indonesian-owned properties, however, most of the 1,000 people who died in the riots were the Javanese Indonesian looters who targeted the Chinese shops, not the Chinese themselves, since the looters were burnt to death in a massive fire.
- May 19
  - The Galaxy IV communications satellite fails, leaving 80–90% of the world's pagers without service.
  - The wreck of the aircraft carrier USS Yorktown, sunk during the Battle of Midway in 1942, is found near Midway Atoll by a team led by former US Navy officer Robert D. Ballard.
- May 21 – Suharto (elected 1967) resigns, after 32 years as President of Indonesia and his 7th consecutive re-election by the Indonesian Parliament (MPR). Suharto's hand-picked Vice President, B. J. Habibie, becomes Indonesia's third president.
- May 26 – Bear Grylls, 23, becomes the youngest British climber to scale Mount Everest.

- May 28 – Nuclear testing: In response to a series of Indian nuclear tests, Pakistan explodes 5 nuclear devices of its own in the Chaghai hills of Baluchistan, codenamed *Chagai-I*, prompting the United States, Japan and other nations to impose economic sanctions. Pakistan celebrates Youm-e-Takbir annually.
- May 30
    - A 6.6 magnitude earthquake hits northern Afghanistan, killing up to 5,000.
    - A second nuclear test, codenamed *Chagai-II*, is conducted and supervised by the Pakistan Atomic Energy Commission (PAEC).

June

- June 2 – The CIH computer virus is discovered in Taiwan.
- June 3 – Eschede train disaster: An Intercity-Express high-speed train derails between Hanover and Hamburg, Germany, causing 101 deaths.
- June 7
    - Former Brigadier-General Ansumane Mané seizes control over military barracks in Bissau, marking the beginning of the Guinea-Bissau Civil War (1998–99).
    - Peter Arnett publishes a false report of Operation Tailwind (initiated 1970), claiming that sarin nerve agents were used to eliminate a group of deserting U.S. soldiers.
    - James Byrd, Jr. is beaten and dragged to death by 3 white men in Jasper, Texas.
- June 9–12 – The 1998 FIFA World Cup begins in France.

- June 12 – The Centennial Celebration of Independence of the Philippines from Spain is observed.
- June 25 – Microsoft releases Windows 98.
- June 30 – Philippine Vice President Joseph Estrada is sworn in as the 13th President of the Philippines.

July

- July 2 – J. K. Rowling's Harry Potter and the Chamber of Secrets is published.
- July 5 – Japan launches a probe to Mars, joining the United States and Russia as an outer space-exploring nation.
- July 6 – The new Hong Kong International Airport at Chek Lap Kok opens, while the historic Kai Tak Airport closes.
- July 12 – France beats Brazil 3–0 in the football World Cup final.
- July 17
    - At a conference in Rome, 120 countries vote to create a permanent International Criminal Court to prosecute individuals for genocide, crimes against humanity, war crimes, and the crime of aggression.
    - In Saint Petersburg, Nicholas II of Russia and his family are buried in St. Catherine Chapel, 80 years after he and his family were killed by the Lenin-led Bolsheviks in 1918.
    - The 7.0 Mw Papua New Guinea earthquake shakes the region near Aitape with a maximum Mercalli intensity of VIII (*Severe*). This submarine earthquake triggered a landslide that caused a destructive tsunami, leaving 2,183–2,700 dead and thousands injured.

- Biologists report in the journal *Science* how they sequenced the genome of the bacterium that causes syphilis, *Treponema pallidum*.
- July 24 – *Saving Private Ryan* premieres in theaters.

August

Aug.7: Nairobi Embassy bombing.

- August 4 – The Second Congo War begins; 3,900,000 people are killed before it ends in 2003, making it the bloodiest war, to date, since World War II.
- August 7
  - Yangtze River Floods: In China the Yangtze river breaks through the main bank; before this, from August 1–5, peripheral levees collapsed consecutively in Jiayu County Baizhou Bay. The death toll exceeds 12,000, with many thousands more injured.
  - 1998 U.S. embassy bombings: The bombings of the United States embassies in Dar es Salaam, Tanzania, and Nairobi, Kenya, kill 224 people and injure over 4,500; they are linked to terrorist Osama bin Laden, an exile of Saudi Arabia.

- August 15 – The Omagh bombing is carried out in Northern Ireland by the Real IRA.
- August 24 – The first RFID human implantation is tested in the United Kingdom.
- August 26 – Computer virus CIH activates and attacks Windows 9x.

September

Canadian Coast Guard Vessel Henry Hudson searches for Swissair Flight 111 debris

- September 2
  - A McDonnell Douglas MD-11 airliner (Swissair Flight 111) crashes near Peggys Cove, Nova Scotia, after taking off from New York City en route to Geneva; all 229 people on board are killed.
  - A United Nations court finds Jean-Paul Akayesu, the former mayor of a small town in Rwanda, guilty of 9 counts of genocide, marking the first time that the 1948 law banning genocide is enforced.
- September 4
  - Google, Inc. is founded in Menlo Park, California, by Stanford University PhD candidates Larry Page and Sergey Brin.

- ○ The last former Soviet Union radar station, Skrunda-1, is closed down in Latvia.
- September 5 – The Government of North Korea adopts a military dictatorship on its 50th anniversary.
- September 10 - At midnight, a shooting occurs aboard an *Akula*-class nuclear-powered attack submarine of the Russian Navy docked in the northern Russian port-city of Severomorsk. The shooter, Alexander Kuzminykh, a 19-year-old seaman from St. Petersburg, opened fire after murdering a soldier (who was supervising his detention on punishment charges in the personnel quarters of the submarine) with a chisel, and taking his AK-74U carbine. After killing five people and wounding one with the dead soldier's weapon, he proceeded to take 2 fellow soldiers hostage, and barricaded himself in the submarine's torpedo room, where he would later murder them. For 23 hours, doctors, relatives, and a priest attempt to persuade him to surrender, but to no avail. After threatening numerous times to set the torpedo room on fire (an event the authorities feared would cause a quote "second Chernobyl"), the crisis came to an end on the morning of 12 September, when a special anti-terrorist commando unit of the Russian Federal Security Service (FSB) launched a raid on the torpedo room during which, Kuzminkykh allegedly committed suicide, contrary to prior reports that he'd been killed by the unit.
- September 12 - The Cuban Five intelligence agents are arrested in Miami, and convicted of espionage. The agents claim they were not spying against the United States Government but against the Cuban exile community in Miami.

- September 24 – Iranian President Mohammad Khatami retracts a fatwa against *Satanic Verses* author Salman Rushdie that was in force since 1989 stating that the Iranian government will "neither support nor hinder assassination operations on Rushdie".

October

- October 2 – *Antz*, the first feature film made by DreamWorks, is released.
- October 6 – Matthew Shepard is beaten and left to die in a cornfield in Laramie, Wyoming.
- October 14 – Eric Rudolph is charged with 4 bombings (including the 1996 Olympic bombing) in Atlanta.
- October 16 – British police place General Augusto Pinochet, the former Chilean dictator from 1973-1990, under house arrest during his medical treatment in the UK.
- October 17 – A pipeline explosion in Jesse, Nigeria results in 1,082 deaths.
- October 29 – Hurricane Mitch makes landfall in Central America, killing an estimated 18,000 people.

November

- November 16 – Sesame Workshop (back then known as **Children's Television Workshop**) launches Elmo's World, the most famous Sesame Street segment, lasting from the late 90' to Sesame Street's 40th anniversary (69-09) and the 10th anniversary of the segment itself (99-09).

- November 17 – *Voyager 1* overtakes *Pioneer 10* as the most distant man-made object from the Solar System, at a distance of 69.419 AU (1.03849×10^{10} km).
- November 20 – A Russian Proton rocket is launched from the Baikonur Cosmodrome in Kazakhstan, carrying the first segment of the International Space Station, the 21-ton Zarya Module.
- November 21 – Nintendo releases The Legend of Zelda: Ocarina of Time.
- November 24 – A declassified report by Swiss IOC official Marc Hodler reveals that bribes had been used to bring the 2002 Winter Olympics to Salt Lake City during bidding process in 1995. The International Olympic Committee, the Salt Lake Organizing Committee, the United States Olympic Committee and the United States Department of Justice immediately launch an investigation into the scandal.

December

- December 4 – The Space Shuttle Endeavour launches the first American component to the International Space Station, the 25,600 lb Unity module on STS-88. It docks with Zarya two days later.
- December 6 – Hugo Chávez, politician and former member of the Venezuelan military, is elected President of Venezuela.
- December 14 – The Yugoslav Army ambushes a column of 140 Kosovo Liberation Army militants attempting to smuggle arms from Albania into Kosovo, killing 36.

- December 16–19 – Iraq disarmament crisis: U.S. President Bill Clinton orders airstrikes on Iraq. UNSCOM withdraws all weapons inspectors from Iraq.
- December 19 – The U.S. House of Representatives forwards articles of impeachment against President Clinton to the Senate, making him the second president to be impeached in the nation.
- December 29 – Khmer Rouge leaders apologize for the post-Vietnam War genocide in Cambodia that claimed over 1 million in the 1970s.
- December 31 – The first leap second since June 30, 1997 occurs. In the eurozone, the currency rates of this day are fixed permanently.

Date unknown

- Ibrahim Hanna, the last native speaker of Mlahsô, dies in Qamishli, Syria, making the language effectively extinct. Also, the last native speaker of related Bijil Neo-Aramaic dies in Jerusalem.
- Italian road racing cyclist Marco Pantani wins both the Tour de France and Giro d'Italia this year.

Births

January

Lara Robinson

Ariel Winter

- January 1
  - March Tian Boedihardjo, Hong Konger child prodigy
  - Samuel Kwong, American sabre fencer
  - Lara Robinson, Australian actress
- January 2

- Chen Xinyi, Chinese swimmer
- Christell, Chilean singer
- January 4
  - Coco Jones, American actress and singer
  - Liza Soberano, Filipino actress and singer
- January 6 – Yuuka Yano, Japanese actress
- January 9
  - Kerris Dorsey, American actress and singer
  - Sean Day, Belgian-born Canadian ice hockey player
- January 10 – Xu Shilin, Chinese tennis player
- January 12 – Nathan Gamble, American actor
- January 13
  - Gabrielle Daleman, Canadian figure skater
  - Kamron Doyle, American ten-pin bowler
- January 14
  - Ai Moritaka, Japanese model and actress
  - Nick Romeo Reimann, German actor
- January 15 – Lidiya Zablotskaya, Belarusian singer
- January 17 – Luca Schuler, Swiss freestyle skier
- January 18 – Alfie McIlwain, English actor
- January 21 – Amelia Hundley, American artistic gymnast
- January 23
  - Rachel Crow, American singer and actress
  - Cole Custer, American stock car racing driver
  - Thomas Meilstrup, Danish singer and actor
  - Silentó American rapper
- January 24 – Eglė Jurgaitytė, Lithuanian singer
- January 26
  - Leeah D. Jackson, American actress
  - Bimal Magar, Nepali footballer

- January 27 – Rebeka Kim, South Korean ice dancer
- January 28 – Ariel Winter, American actress
- January 29 – Mion Mukaichi, Japanese idol, singer, and actress
- January 30 – Jordana Beatty, Australian actress

February

Matthew Davidson

- February 3 – Michael McLeod, Canadian ice hockey player
- February 4 – Scott Jones, English paralympic athlete
- February 5 – Sreelakshmi Suresh, Indian web designer
- February 7 – Angelique Sabrina, Bahamian singer-songwriter, dancer and actress
- February 8 – Šarlote Lēnmane, Latvian singer
- February 10
    - Gray Gaulding, American stock car racing driver
    - Candy Hsu, Taiwanese singer-songwriter, actress and record producer
- February 12 – Chen Siyi, Chinese gymnast
- February 15 – Zachary Gordon, American actor
- February 16
    - Kim Su-ji, South Korean diver

- ○ Seo Young-joo, South Korean actor
- February 18 – Matthew Davidson, American guitarist
- February 19 – Sam Kim, Korean-American singer and guitarist
- February 20 – Matt Hunter Correa, American singer and voice actor
- February 26 – Isaac Durnford, Canadian actor
- February 27 – Theo Stevenson, English actor

March

Satoko Miyahara

- March 1 – Tengku Muhammad Ismail of Terengganu
- March 9 – Kaylin Whitney, American sprinter
- March 10 – Nicholas Nip, American chess champion
- March 12
  - ○ Annaleise Carr, Canadian swimmer
  - ○ Jordan Jansen, Australian singer
  - ○ Alina Müller, Swiss ice hockey player
  - ○ Elizaveta Ukolova, Czech figure skater
- March 13 – Oliver Stokes, English actor
- March 14 – Szuyu Rachel Su, Taiwanese classical pianist

- March 17 – Nathan O'Toole, Irish actor
- March 18 – Sergei Chernousov, Russian footballer
- March 19 – Sakura Miyawaki, Japanese singer
- March 22 – Harsh Mayar, Indian actor
- March 24 – Isabel Suckling, English singer
- March 25 – Ryan Simpkins, American actress
- March 26
  - Daria Grushina, Russian ski jumper
  - Satoko Miyahara, Japanese figure skater
- March 27 – BJ Forbes, Filipino actor
- March 29
  - Kim Tae-kyung, South Korean figure skater
  - Shealeigh, American singer-songwriter
- March 30 – Janella Salvador, Filipina actress and singer
- March 31
  - Jakob Chychrun, American ice hockey player
  - Anna Seidel, German short track speed skater
  - Valeria Gorlats, Estonian tennis player

April

Peyton List

Elle Fanning

- April 1 – Isabella Bliss, Australian chef
- April 3 – Paris Jackson, American television personality and actress
- April 4 – Malcolm Sutherland-Foggio, American philanthropist
- April 5 – Kaito Nakamura, Japanese actor and model
- April 6
    - Rina Katsuta, Japanese singer
    - Peyton List, American actress
    - Spencer List, American actor
- April 9 – Elle Fanning, American actress
- April 10 - Anna Pogorilaya, Russian figure skater
- April 11 – Oliver Dillon, English actor
- April 16 – Paul Salas, Filipino actor
- April 18 – Joyce Tafatatha, Malawian swimmer
- April 24 – Ryan Newman, American actress
- April 26 – Jan-Krzysztof Duda, Polish chess Grandmaster
- April 29 – Kimberly Birrell, German-born Australian tennis player

May

Tornado Alicia Black

- May 2 – Vasilisa Davankova, Russian pair skater
- May 4 – Taylar Hender, American actress
- May 6
    - Andranik Alexanyan, Ukrainian singer-songwriter
    - Lil Poison, American professional gamer
    - Kayden Troff, American chess champion
- May 12 – Tornado Alicia Black, American tennis player
- May 13 – Karen Iwata, Japanese singer and voice actress
- May 14 – Taruni Sachdev, Indian actress (d. 2012)
- May 16
    - Adian Pitkeev, Russian figure skater
    - Ariel Waller, Canadian actress
- May 18
    - Polina Edmunds, American figure skater
    - Brianna Fruean, Samoan environmental activist
- May 20 – Nam Nguyen, Canadian figure skater
- May 21 – Gabbie Rae, American singer
- May 22 – Carmel Buckingham, Slovak singer-songwriter
- May 26

- Vladimir Arzumanyan, Armenian singer
- Shannon, English-born South Korean singer
- May 28 – Riho Sayashi, Japanese singer
- May 29
  - Lucía Gil, Spanish singer and actress
  - Oliver Stokes, British actor

June

Yulia Lipnitskaya

Suzu Hirose

- June 1 – Aleksandra Soldatova, Russian rhythmic gymnast

- June 5 – Yulia Lipnitskaya, Russian figure skater
- June 6 – Anna Shershak, Russian figure skater
- June 7 – Graham Newberry, British-American figure skater
- June 8 – Arjun Ayyangar, American pianist and child prodigy
- June 11 – Charlie Tahan, American actor
- June 13 – Abdallah El Akal, Israeli actor
- June 14
  - Julia Joyce, English actress
  - Daniel-Leon Kit, American actor
  - Taishi Nakagawa, Japanese actor and model
- June 15
  - Rachel Covey, American actress
  - Tanner Maguire, American actor
  - Alexander Samarin, Russian figure skater
- June 16 – Veronica Hults, American artistic gymnast
- June 19
  - Suzu Hirose, Japanese actress and model
  - Joey Jett, American skateboarder
  - Atticus Shaffer, American actor
  - Viktoria Solnceva, Ukrainian swimmer
- June 20 – Jadin Gould, American actress
- June 23 – Folarin Ogunsola, Gambian swimmer
- June 24 – Coy Stewart, American actor

July

Jaden Smith

Madison Pettis

- July 2 – Ema Klinec, Slovenian ski jumper
- July 4 – Malia Obama, daughter of U.S. President Barack Obama
- July 7 – Dylan Sprayberry, American actor
- July 8
  - Jaden Smith, American actor
  - Daria Spiridonova, Russian artistic gymnast
- July 9
  - Robert Capron, American actor

- Tiger Onitsuka, Japanese drummer
- July 10
  - Haley Pullos, American actress
  - Hollie Steel, English singer
- July 12 – Swini Khara, Indian actress
- July 15 – Spencir Bridges, American actor
- July 17
  - Don Felipe of Spain
  - Shione Sawada, Japanese actress
  - Lilli Schweiger, German actress
- July 18 – Nixzmary Brown, American child abuse victim (d. 2006)
- July 19 – Lil Woods, English actress
- July 20 – Sinead Michael, English actress
- July 22
  - Alicia Moffet, Canadian singer
  - Madison Pettis, American actress
- July 24 – Bindi Irwin, Australian actress and television presenter, daughter of Steve Irwin
- July 26 – Maya Sakura, Japanese singer and actress
- July 28
  - Sasha Meneghel, Brazilian volleyball player, model and actress
  - Jackson Murphy, American movie critic
- July 30 – Johnny Bennett, English-born Irish actor
- July 31 – Rico Rodriguez, American actor

August

Shawn Mendes

China Anne McClain

- August 1 – Khamani Griffin, American actor
- August 3 – Cozi Zuehlsdorff, American actress, pianist and singer
- August 5
    - Kanon Suzuki, Japanese singer
    - Ana-Maria Yanakieva, Bulgarian singer
    - Mimi Keene, English actress
- August 6 – Jack Scanlon, English actor
- August 7 – Felicia Hano, American artistic gymnast
- August 8

- o Ronan Parke, English singer
- o Shawn Mendes, Canadian singer
- August 10 – Diptayan Ghosh, Indian chess champion
- August 11 – Nadia Azzi, American classical pianist
- August 13
  - o Arina Averina, Russian rhythmic gymnast
  - o Dina Averina, Russian rhythmic gymnast
  - o Dalma Gálfi, Hungarian tennis player
  - o Devan Leos, American actor
- August 14 – Amy Marren, English paralympic swimmer
- August 15 – Gulliver McGrath, Australian actor
- August 16 – Rachel Traets, Dutch singer
- August 18 – Cakka Nuraga, Indonesian musician and singer
- August 19 – Ella Guevara, Filipina actress
- August 21 - Prince Villanueva, Filipino, actor
- August 24 – Robin, Finnish singer
- August 25
  - o Abraham Mateo, Spanish actor and singer
  - o China Anne McClain, American actress and singer
- August 28 – Haruka Fukuhara, Japanese singer

September

Richard Wang

- September 1 – Emily Condon, Australian footballer
- September 3 – Amey Pandya, Indian actress
- September 6 – Michele Perniola, Italian singer
- September 9 – Shannon Matthews, English kidnap victim
- September 11
    - Makenna Cowgill, American actress
    - Jacky Wong, Hong Konger actor
- September 17 – Richard Wang, Canadian chess champion
- September 21 - Miguel Tanfelix, Filipino actor
- September 24 – Chandler Frantz, American actor
- September 26 – Ivan Pavlov, Ukrainian figure skater
- September 28
    - Aleksandra Goryachkina, Russian chess Grandmaster
    - Gotita de Plata, Mexican wrestler
    - Jenna Rose, American singer
- September 30 – Trevor Moran, American singer and YouTube personality

October

Nolan Gould

- October 2 – Maxime Godart, French actor
- October 10 – Nash Aguas, Filipino actor
- October 12 – Tyler Pierce, American figure skater
- October 18 – Monica Avanesyan, Armenian singer
- October 19 – Yang Dingxin, Chinese Go player
- October 20 – Jordan Allan, Scottish footballer
- October 23 – Amandla Stenberg, American actress
- October 24 – Daya, American singer
- October 25 – Guan Tianlang, Chinese golfer
- October 28
  - Nolan Gould, American actor
  - Perrine Laffont, French mogul skier
- October 29
  - Prince Constantine Alexios of Greece and Denmark
  - Maria Kharenkova, Russian artistic gymnast
  - Lance Stroll, Canadian racing driver
- October 30 – Meimi Tamura, Japanese singer and actress
- October 31 – Alice Morel-Michaud, Canadian actress

November

Bradley Steven Perry

- November 3
  - Maddison Elliott, Australian paralympic swimmer
  - Novemthree Siahaan, Indonesian gigantiform cementoma victim (d. 2005)
- November 4 – Darcy Rose Byrnes, American actress and singer-songwriter
- November 7 – Octavio Ocaña, Mexican actor
- November 10 – Renz Valerio, Filipino actor
- November 11
  - Ruby Jerins, American actress
  - Carlo Lacana, Filipino actor
- November 13
  - Gattlin Griffith, American actor
  - Charlie Storwick, Canadian singer-songwriter and actress
- November 16 – Priyanshi Somani, Indian mental calculator
- November 17 – Kara Hayward, American actress
- November 20 – Savannah Robinson, American singer
- November 23 – Bradley Steven Perry, American actor
- November 24
  - Brecken Palmer, American actor

- ○ Bridger Palmer, American actor
- November 25 – Shin Dong-woo, South Korean actor
- November 28 – Dylan Bluestone, American actor
- November 29 – Ayumu Hirano, Japanese snowboarder

December

Reece Oxford

Martin Ødegaard

Gianina Ernst

- December 2
  - Annalise Basso, American actress
  - Amber Montana, American actress
- December 4 – Si Yajie, Chinese diver
- December 6 – Angelīna Kučvaļska, Latvian figure skater
- December 8
  - Ebuka Chukwu, American citizen, one of the Chukwu octuplets
  - Anastasia Rizikov, Canadian classical pianist
- December 11 – Gabz, British singer
- December 14
  - Maude Apatow, American actress
  - Maggie Voisin, American freestyle skier
- December 15 – Chandler Canterbury, American actor
- December 16
  - Kiara Muhammad, American actress and singer
  - Reece Oxford, English footballer
- December 17 – Martin Ødegaard, Norwegian footballer
- December 18 – Erhan Can Kartal, Turkish actor
- December 18 – Alejandro Felipe, Mexican actor

- December 19 – Frans Jeppsson-Wall, Swedish singer
- December 20
  - Chidi, Echerem, Chima, Odera, Ikem, Jioke and Gorom Chukwu, American citizens, seven of the Chukwu octuplets (Odera d. December 27)
  - Ivett Tóth, Hungarian figure skater
- December 22 – G. Hannelius, American actress
- December 24 – Nikita Howarth, New Zealand paralympic swimmer
- December 26 – Kesz Váldez, Filipino humanitarian
- December 28 – Jared Gilman, American actor
- December 29 – Seamus Davey-Fitzpatrick, American actor
- December 31 – Gianina Ernst, German ski jumper

Deaths

January

Vladimir Prelog

Carl Perkins

- January 1 – Helen Wills Moody, American tennis player (b. 1905)
- January 2 – Feodor I. Kozhevnikov, Soviet legal expert (b. 1893)
- January 4 –
  - Mae Questel, American actress (b. 1908)
  - Carlo Ludovico Bragaglia, Italian film director (b. 1894)
- January 5 – Sonny Bono, American singer, actor, and politician (b. 1935)
- January 7 – Vladimir Prelog, Croatian chemist, Nobel laureate (b. 1906)
- January 8 – Michael Tippett, English composer (b. 1905)
- January 9 – Kenichi Fukui, Japanese chemist, Nobel Prize laureate (b. 1918)
- January 11
  - Ellis Rabb, American director and actor (b. 1930)
  - Klaus Tennstedt, German conductor (b. 1926)
- January 12
  - Kyle W. Dinkheller, American policeman (b. 1975)
  - Phyllis Nelson, American singer (b. 1950)

- January 15 – Junior Wells, American harmonica player (b. 1934)
- January 16
    - Emil Sitka, American actor (b. 1914)
    - Hermann Wedekind, artistic director Festspiele Balver Höhle (b. 1910)
- January 18 – Monica Edwards, British writer (b. 1912)
- January 19 – Carl Perkins, American guitarist (b. 1932)
- January 21 – Jack Lord, American actor (b. 1920)
- January 23 – Alfredo Ormando, Italian writer (b. 1958)
- January 26 – Shinichi Suzuki (violinist), inventor of the international Suzuki music education (b. 1898)
- January 28 – Shotaro Ishinomori, Japanese Manga artist, "Father of Henshin heroes" (b. 1938)

February

Ernst Jünger

- February 2
    - Haroun Tazieff, French volcanologist and geologist (b. 1914)

- o Raymond Cattell, British and American psychologist (b. 1905)
- February 3
  - o Fat Pat, American rapper (b. 1970)
  - o Karla Faye Tucker, Texas murderer (b. 1959)
- February 6
  - o Falco, Austrian musician (b. 1957)
  - o Carl Wilson, American musician (The Beach Boys) (b. 1946)
  - o Nazim al-Kudsi, former President and Prime Minister of Syria (b. 1906)
- February 7
  - o Lawrence Sanders, American author (b. 1920)
  - o Roger Nicholas Angleton, American murderer (b. 1942)
- February 8
  - o Halldór Laxness, Icelandic writer, Nobel Prize laureate (b. 1902)
  - o Enoch Powell, British politician (b. 1912)
  - o Julian Lincoln Simon, American economist and author (b. 1932)
- February 9 – Maurice Schumann, former French Minister of Foreign Affairs (b. 1911)
- February 11 – Jonathan Hole, American actor (b. 1904)
- February 16 – Fernando Abril Martorell, former Spanish Deputy Prime Minister (b. 1936)
- February 17
  - o Ernst Jünger, German writer (b. 1895)
  - o Bob Merrill, American composer and screenwriter (b. 1921)

- February 18 – Harry Caray, American television and radio broadcaster (b. 1917)
- February 22
  - Red Reeder, U.S. Army officer and author (b. 1902)
  - Abraham Alexander Ribicoff, American Democratic Party politician (b. 1910)
  - Athol Rowan, South African cricketer (b. 1921)
  - José María de Areilza, former Spanish Minister of Foreign Affairs (b. 1909)
- February 23
  - Raman Lamba, Indian cricketer (b. 1960)
  - Sean A. Moore, American writer (b. 1965)
- February 24 – Henny Youngman, English-born comedian (b. 1906)
- February 26 – Theodore Schultz, American economist, Nobel Prize laureate (b. 1902)
- February 27
  - George H. Hitchings, American scientist, recipient of the Nobel Prize in Physiology or Medicine (b. 1905)
  - J. T. Walsh, American actor (b. 1943)
- February 28
  - Todd Duncan, American opera singer (b. 1903)
  - Dermot Morgan, Irish actor and comedian (b. 1952)

March

Lloyd Bridges

Hans von Ohain

- March 2 – Darcy O'Brien, American author (b. 1939)
- March 3 – Fred W. Friendly, American television journalist and executive (b. 1915)
- March 7 – Bernarr Rainbow, historian of music education, organist, and choir master, (b. 1914)
- March 8 – Ray Nitschke, American football player (b. 1936)
- March 10 – Lloyd Bridges, American actor (b. 1913)
- March 12
    - Judge Dread, English musician (b. 1945)
    - Beatrice Wood, American artist and ceramicist (b. 1893)
    - Jozef Kroner, Slovak actor (*The Shop on Main Street*) (b. 1924)
- March 13
    - Bill Reid, Canadian artist (b. 1920)

- Risen Star, American racehorse (b. 1985)
- Hans von Ohain, German physicist, and designer of the first operational jet engine (b. 1911)
- March 15
  - Benjamin Spock, American athlete, pediatrician, and author (b. 1903)
  - Dušan Pašek, Slovak ice hockey player (b. 1960)
- March 16 – Derek Barton, British chemist, Nobel Prize laureate (b. 1918)
- March 20 – George Howard, American jazz saxophone musician (b. 1956)
- March 25 – Daniel Massey, English actor (b. 1933)
- March 27 – Ferdinand Anton Ernst Porsche, Austrian auto designer and businessman (b. 1909)
- March 31 – Bella Abzug, American politician (b. 1920)

April

Pol Pot

Octavio Paz

- April 1
    - Gene Evans, American actor (b. 1920)
    - Rozz Williams, American singer (b. 1963)
- April 2 – Rob Pilatus, member of the pop group Milli Vanilli (b.circa 1966)
- April 3 – Charles Lang, American cinematographer (b. 1901)
- April 5 – Cozy Powell, English rock drummer (b. 1947)
- April 6
    - Wendy O. Williams, American singer (b. 1949)
    - Tammy Wynette, American singer (b. 1942)
- April 11 – Rodney Harvey, American actor and model (b. 1967)
- April 13 – Patrick de Gayardon, French skydiver and skysurfing pioneer (b. 1960)
- April 15
    - Rose Maddox, American singer (b. 1925)
    - Pol Pot, Cambodian Khmer Rouge leader (b. 1925)
- April 16
    - Fred Davis, English snooker player (b. 1913)

- Marie-Louise Meilleur, Canadian supercentenarian (b. 1880)
- April 17
  - Linda McCartney, American photographer and musician and wife of former Beatle Paul McCartney (b. 1941)
  - Muhammad Metwally Al Shaarawy, Egyptian Muslim jurist (b. 1911)
- April 19 – Octavio Paz, Mexican diplomat and writer, Nobel Prize laureate (b. 1914)
- April 21
  - Peter Lind Hayes, American entertainer (b. 1915)
  - Irene Vernon, American actress (b. 1922)
- April 22 – Kitch Christie, South African rugby coach (b. 1940)
- April 23
  - Konstantinos Karamanlis, Greek politician (b. 1907)
  - James Earl Ray, American assassin (b. 1928)
- April 25
  - Christian Mortensen, Danish supercentenarian (b. 1882)
  - Wright Morris, American photographer and writer (b. 1910)
- April 26 – Joan Mary Wayne Brown, British author who the pseudonyms Mary Gervaise, Hilary Wayne and Bellamy Brown (b. 1906)
- April 27
  - Carlos Castaneda, Peruvian-born American anthropologist and author (b. 1925)
  - Anne Desclos, French writer (b. 1907)

May

Alice Faye

Frank Sinatra

Phil Hartman

- May 1 – Eldridge Cleaver, American activist (b. 1935)

- May 2
  - Kevin Lloyd, British actor (b. 1949)
  - Justin Fashanu, British footballer (b. 1961)
  - hide, Japanese musician (b. 1964)
  - Gene Raymond, American actor (b. 1908)
- May 7
  - Allan McLeod Cormack, South African–born physicist, recipient of the Nobel Prize in Physiology or Medicine (b. 1924)
  - Eddie Rabbitt, American musician (b. 1941)
- May 9 – Alice Faye, American entertainer (b. 1915)
- May 14
  - Frank Sinatra, American entertainer (b. 1915)
  - Marjory Stoneman Douglas, American conservationist and writer (b. 1890)
- May 15 – Earl Manigault, American basketball player (b. 1944)
- May 19 – Sōsuke Uno, Prime Minister of Japan (b. 1922)
- May 22
  - John Derek, American actor and film director (b. 1926)
  - José Enrique Moyal, mathematical physicist (b. 1910)
- May 28 –
  - Phil Hartman, Canadian-born American artist, writer, actor, and comedian (b. 1948)
  - Philip L. Carret, investor and founder (in 1928) of Pioneer Fund (b. 1896)
- May 29 – Barry Goldwater, American politician (b. 1909)

June

Maureen O'Sullivan

- June 1 – Darwin Joston, American actor (b. 1937)
- June 2
    - Junkyard Dog, American pro wrestler (b. 1952)
    - Dorothy Stickney, American actress (b. 1896)
- June 3 – Poul Bundgaard, Danish actor and singer (b. 1922)
- June 5 – Jeanette Nolan, American actress (b. 1911)
- June 8
    - Sani Abacha, President of Nigeria (b. 1943)
    - Jackie McGlew, South African cricketer (b. 1929)
- June 10 – Hammond Innes, English author (b. 1914)
- June 11 – Catherine Cookson, English author (b. 1906)
- June 12 – Theresa Merritt, American actress (b. 1924)
- June 13 – Birger Ruud, Norwegian athlete (b. 1911)
- June 20 – Conrad Schumann, East German border guard (b. 1942)
- June 22 – Benny Green, British writer, radio broadcaster and saxophonist (b. 1927)
- June 23 – Maureen O'Sullivan, Irish actress (b. 1911)
- June 25 – Lounès Matoub, Berber Kabyle singer (b. 1956)

- June 27 – Kerim Tekin, Turkish pop singer and actor (b. 1975)
- June 28 – Marion Eugene Carl, U.S. Marine Corps World War II fighter ace and test pilot (b. 1915)

July

Alan Shepard

- July 3 – Danielle Bunten Berry, American software developer (b. 1949)
- July 5
    - Sid Luckman, American football player (b. 1916)
    - Johnny Speight, British television scriptwriter (b. 1920)
- July 6 – Roy Rogers, American singer and actor (b. 1911)
- July 12 – Arkady Ostashev, Soviet engineer and rocket scientist (b. 1925)
- July 17 – Joseph Maher, Irish actor (b. 1933)
- July 19 – Elmer Valo, Slovak Major League Baseball player (b. 1921)
- July 21
    - Alan Shepard, American astronaut (b. 1923)

- ○ Robert Young, American actor (b. 1907)
- July 22 – Hermann Prey, German bass-baritone (b. 1929)
- July 27 – Binnie Barnes, English actress (b. 1903)
- July 28 – Harvie Branscomb, the fourth chancellor of Vanderbilt University from 1946 to 1963 (b. 1894)
- July 29 – Jerome Robbins, American choreographer and director (b. 1918)
- July 30
  - ○ Buffalo Bob Smith, American children's television host (b. 1917)
  - ○ Jorge Russek, Mexican actor (b. 1932)
- July 31 – Sylvia Field, American actress (*Mrs. Wilson*; Dennis the Menace)

August

- August 1 – Eva Bartok, Hungarian actress (b. 1927)
- August 2 – Shari Lewis, American ventriloquist (b. 1933)
- August 3 – Alfred Schnittke, Russian-born composer (b. 1934)
- August 4 – Yury Artyukhin, cosmonaut (b. 1930)
- August 5 – Todor Zhivkov, former President of Bulgaria (b. 1911)
- August 6 – André Weil, French mathematician (b. 1906)
- August 9 – Frankie Ruiz, Puerto Rican singer (b. 1958)
- August 13 – Julien Green, French-born American writer (b. 1900)
- August 24 – E. G. Marshall, American actor (b. 1910)
- August 25 – Lewis F. Powell, Jr., American Justice of the Supreme Court (b. 1907)

- August 26 – Frederick Reines, American physicist, Nobel Prize laureate (b. 1918)

September

George Wallace

Betty Carter

- September 1 – Cary Middlecoff, American golfer (b. 1921)
- September 2
    - Jackie Blanchflower, Irish footballer (b. 1933)
    - Allen Drury, American writer (b. 1918)
    - Walter L. Morgan, founder of the Wellington Fund, (b. 1898)

- September 5
  - Fernando Balzaretti, Mexican actor (b. 1946)
  - Leo Penn, American actor and director (b. 1921)
- September 6 – Akira Kurosawa, Japanese screenwriter, producer, and director (b. 1910)
- September 8 – Leonid Kinskey, Russian-born actor (b. 1903)
- September 9 – Lucio Battisti, Italian singer (b. 1943)
- September 10 – Carl Forgione, British actor (b. 1944)
- September 11 – Dane Clark, American actor (b. 1912)
- September 13 – George Wallace, American politician (b. 1919)
- September 14
  - Johnny Adams, American musician (b. 1932)
  - Yang Shangkun, former President of the People's Republic of China (b. 1907)
- September 17 – Gustav Nezval, Czech actor (b. 1907)
- September 20 – Muriel Humphrey, wife of Vice President Hubert Humphrey (b. 1912)
- September 21 – Florence "Flo-Jo" Griffith-Joyner, American runner (b. 1959)
- September 23 – Mary Frann, American actress (b. 1943)
- September 26 – Betty Carter, American jazz singer (b. 1929)
- September 27 – Narita Brian, Japanese racehorse (b. 1991)
- September 29 – Herbert V. Prochnow, U.S. banking executive, noted toastmaster, and author (b. 1897)
- September 30
  - Dan Quisenberry, baseball player (b. 1953)
  - Bruno Munari, Italian-born industrial designer (b. 1907)
  - Pavel Štěpán, Czech pianist (b. 1925)
  - Robert Lewis Taylor, American author (b. 1912)

October

Roddy McDowall

- October 2
  - Gene Autry, American actor, singer, and sports team owner (b. 1907)
  - Olivier Gendebien, Belgian race car driver (b. 1924)
- October 3 – Roddy McDowall, British actor (b. 1928)
- October 6 –
  - Mark Belanger, American baseball player (b. 1944)
  - Ambrose Burke, English professor and Catholic priest (b. 1895)
- October 8 – Zhang Chongren, Chinese artist (b. 1907)
- October 9 – Ian Johnson, Australian cricketer (b. 1917)
- October 10 – Tommy Quaid, Irish hurler (b. 1957)
- October 11 – Richard Denning, American actor (b. 1914)
- October 12 – Matthew Shepard, American murder victim (b. 1976)
- October 13 – General Gérard Charles Édouard Thériault, Canadian Chief of the Defence Staff (b. 1932)
- October 14 – Frankie Yankovic, American musician (b. 1916)
- October 16 – Jon Postel, American Internet pioneer (b. 1943)

- October 19 – Germán List Arzubide, Mexican poet and revolutionary (b. 1898)
- October 17
  - Joan Hickson, British actress (b. 1906)
  - Hakim Mohammed Said, Pakistani scholar and philanthropist (b. 1920)
- October 22 – Eric Ambler, British writer (b. 1909)
- October 28
  - Ghulam Ahmed, Indian former cricket captain (b. 1922)
  - James Goldman, American writer (b. 1927)
- October 29 – Ted Hughes, English poet (b. 1930)

November

Jean Marais

- November 3 – Bob Kane, American comic book creator (b. 1915)
- November 8 – Jean Marais, French actor (b. 1913)
- November 10
  - Hal Newhouser, baseball player (b. 1921)
  - Mary Millar, British actress (b. 1936)

- November 13
  - Valerie Hobson, English actress (b. 1917)
  - Michel Trudeau, Canadian outdoorsman, son of Pierre Trudeau (b. 1975)
  - Doug Wright, English cricketer (b. 1914)
- November 17
  - Kenneth McDuff, American serial killer (b. 1946)
  - Esther Rolle, American actress (b. 1920)
- November 19 – Alan J. Pakula, American film director (b. 1928)
- November 22 – Stu Ungar, professional poker player (b. 1953)
- November 25 – Flip Wilson, American actor and comedian (b. 1933)
- November 28 – Kerry Wendell Thornley, American counterculture figure and writer (b. 1938)
- November 29
  - Martin Ruane, British wrestler best known as Giant Haystacks and later, The Loch Ness Monster (b. 1947)
  - Frank Latimore, American actor (b. 1925)
- November 30 – Margaret Walker, American poet (b. 1915)

December

Martin Rodbell

Norman Fell

Alan Lloyd Hodgkin

- December 1 – Freddie Young, American cinematographer (b. 1902)
- December 2
    - Mikio Oda, Japanese athlete (b. 1905)
    - Brian Stonehouse, English painter and World War II secret agent (b. 1918)
- December 5 – Hazel Bishop, American chemist and inventor of "no-smear" lipstick (b. 1906)
- December 6 – César Baldaccini, French sculptor (b. 1921)
- December 7
    - Michael Craze, British actor (b. 1942)

- Martin Rodbell, American scientist, recipient of the Nobel Prize in Physiology or Medicine (b. 1925)
- December 11 – Lynn Strait, vocalist for band Snot (b. 1968)
- December 12 – Lawton Chiles, U.S. Senator from Florida and Governor of Florida (b. 1930)
- December 13 – Lew Grade, British impresario (b. 1906)
- December 14
  - Norman Fell, American actor (b. 1924)
  - Annette Strauss, American philanthropist and mayor of Dallas, Texas (b. 1924)
- December 16 – William Gaddis, American writer (b. 1922)
- December 17 – Claudia Benton, Peruvian-born child psychologist (b. 1959)
- December 18 – Lev Dyomin, cosmonaut (b. 1926)
- December 19
  - Nelly's, Greek female photographer (b. 1899)
  - Antonio Ordóñez, Spanish bullfighter (b. 1932)
- December 20
  - Irene Hervey, American actress (b. 1910)
  - Alan Lloyd Hodgkin, British scientist, recipient of the Nobel Prize in Physiology or Medicine (b. 1914)
- December 21 – Roger Avon, British actor (b. 1914)
- December 22 – Michelle Thomas, American actress (b. 1969)
- December 23 – David Manners, Canadian-American actor (b. 1900)
- December 25 – John Pulman, English snooker player (b. 1923)
- December 26 – Hurd Hatfield, American actor (b. 1917)
- December 27 – Odera Chukwu, American citizen, one of the Chukwu octuplets (b. December 20)

- December 28 – Robert Rosen, American biologist (b. 1934)
- December 30
  - Keisuke Kinoshita, Japanese film director (b. 1912)
  - George Webb, British actor (b. 1911)

Nobel Prizes

- Physics – Robert B. Laughlin, Horst L. Störmer, Daniel Chee Tsui
- Chemistry – Walter Kohn, John Pople
- Medicine – Robert F. Furchgott, Louis J. Ignarro, Ferid Murad
- Literature – José Saramago
- Peace – John Hume and David Trimble
- Bank of Sweden Prize in Economic Sciences in Memory of Alfred Nobel – Amartya Sen

In the News.

An earthquake measuring 6.1 on the Richter scale kills more than 5,000 people in northeast Afghanistan.

The 1998 Winter Olympics are held in Nagano, Japan.

George Michael is arrested in a public toilet at Will Rogers Memorial Park, California, for committing a lewd act in front of a police officer.

Frank Sinatra, American entertainer (b. 1915) dies.

Bear Grylls, 23, becomes the youngest British climber to scale the top of Mount Everest.

France defeats Brazil 3-0 to win the 1998 FIFA World Cup.

Sky Digital launches in the United Kingdom.

Google Inc. is founded by Stanford University Ph.D. candidates Larry Page and Sergey Brin.

Europeans agree on a single currency the **Euro**.

President Bill Clinton Impeached for perjury and obstruction of justice.

Microsoft becomes biggest Company in the World valued at $261bn on the New York Stock Exchange.

Windows 98 released by Microsoft.

Apple Computer unveils the **iMac.**

Popular Films – Armageddon, Titanic,Saving Private Ryan, Godzilla.

1998 Calendar

January 1998
Sun	Mon	Tue	Wed	Thu	Fri	Sat
				1	2	3
4	5	6	7	8	9	10
11	12	13	14	15	16	17
18	19	20	21	22	23	24
25	26	27	28	29	30	31

February 1998
Sun	Mon	Tue	Wed	Thu	Fri	Sat
1	2	3	4	5	6	7
8	9	10	11	12	13	14
15	16	17	18	19	20	21
22	23	24	25	26	27	28

March 1998
Sun	Mon	Tue	Wed	Thu	Fri	Sat
1	2	3	4	5	6	7
8	9	10	11	12	13	14
15	16	17	18	19	20	21
22	23	24	25	26	27	28
29	30	31				

April 1998
Sun	Mon	Tue	Wed	Thu	Fri	Sat
			1	2	3	4
5	6	7	8	9	10	11
12	13	14	15	16	17	18
19	20	21	22	23	24	25
26	27	28	29	30		

May 1998
Sun	Mon	Tue	Wed	Thu	Fri	Sat
					1	2
3	4	5	6	7	8	9
10	11	12	13	14	15	16
17	18	19	20	21	22	23
24	25	26	27	28	29	30
31						

June 1998
Sun	Mon	Tue	Wed	Thu	Fri	Sat
	1	2	3	4	5	6
7	8	9	10	11	12	13
14	15	16	17	18	19	20
21	22	23	24	25	26	27
28	29	30				

July 1998
Sun	Mon	Tue	Wed	Thu	Fri	Sat
			1	2	3	4
5	6	7	8	9	10	11
12	13	14	15	16	17	18
19	20	21	22	23	24	25
26	27	28	29	30	31	

August 1998
Sun	Mon	Tue	Wed	Thu	Fri	Sat
						1
2	3	4	5	6	7	8
9	10	11	12	13	14	15
16	17	18	19	20	21	22
23	24	25	26	27	28	29
30	31					

September 1998
Sun	Mon	Tue	Wed	Thu	Fri	Sat
		1	2	3	4	5
6	7	8	9	10	11	12
13	14	15	16	17	18	19
20	21	22	23	24	25	26
27	28	29	30			

October 1998
Sun	Mon	Tue	Wed	Thu	Fri	Sat
				1	2	3
4	5	6	7	8	9	10
11	12	13	14	15	16	17
18	19	20	21	22	23	24
25	26	27	28	29	30	31

November 1998
Sun	Mon	Tue	Wed	Thu	Fri	Sat
1	2	3	4	5	6	7
8	9	10	11	12	13	14
15	16	17	18	19	20	21
22	23	24	25	26	27	28
29	30					

December 1998
Sun	Mon	Tue	Wed	Thu	Fri	Sat
		1	2	3	4	5
6	7	8	9	10	11	12
13	14	15	16	17	18	19
20	21	22	23	24	25	26
27	28	29	30	31		

www.ingramcontent.com/pod-product-compliance
Lightning Source LLC
Chambersburg PA
CBHW071119280526
45787CB00003B/1102